RANSOM STREET

Here's what people are saying about
RANSOM STREET

"Imagine a little girl at the beach with a third-degree sunburn. It is raining and she and has been wrapped in a wet sheet. Later she will recall that she as she walked over the dunes, the pain had rendered her "awake in every nerve." That phrase ends the opening poem in Claire Millikin's stunning new collection, RANSOM STREET, and it sounds the key notes of a book that tells in sharpened lyric moments the story of a young woman's coming of age in the face of violence, violation, homelessness, utter alone-ness. But, as the episodes unfold, and the pain is recalled and endured, there emerges from the corner of our eyes an image of a woman who has all along been forging her own fully-realized self and the voice thereof. Keats called our suffering a "vale of soul-making." Down in that valley is where we find Ransom Street and this poetry of every wakened nerve."
—**Fred Marchant, author of** *Said Not Said: Poems* **(2017)**

"'I took up this music, swept thin,' writes Claire Millikin in RANSOM STREET. These poems stand as lithe and learned testimonies to a girlhood bruised by rejection, hunger, abuse, and neglect. 'Then, at last, tell the truth. All of it,' she commands herself, and as she speaks, she enriches us." —**Lynn Levin, author of** *Miss Plastique* **(2013)**

"'Silence is all we dread,' writes Millikin's soul-sister Emily Dickinson, 'There's Ransom in a Voice.' Writing into and out of childhood's mythic terror, in which so much goes unspoken because so much is imperfectly understood, in RANSOM STREET, Millikin believes that 'paper when it's blank / shapes a soul.' One price these poems pay comes from their giving voice to the inchoate anomie of girl-dom. By turns darkly humorous—'Garments do not last / unless knit of Orlon'—and ruthless ('I turned, like a child from its mother / done with love'), the poems are full of starvation, indictment, and a linguistic-emotional courage that risks taking language as far as it can go toward conditional illumination. 'A word,' Millikin writes in 'Holy, Unholy,' 'says most at its breaking point.'" —**Lisa Russ Spaar, author of** *Satin Cash: Poems* **(2008) and** *Orexia: Poems* **(2018)**

"Claire Millikin's poems exhibit how vulnerability is strength, and how memory can sometimes prop us upright. In RANSOM STREET, Millikin claims 'A book is ephemeral, built of names, or numbers,' but I say these poems are built from wind, the tangled networks of roots relaying messages to each other like trees, and 'a boat of language' kept afloat by the tenacity of craft." —**Tara Betts, author of** *Break the Habit* **(2016)**

Ransom Street

POEMS BY CLAIRE MILLIKIN

Introduction by Kathleen Ellis

FLORIDA ■ NEW YORK
www.2leafpress.org

P.O. Box 4378
Grand Central Station
New York, New York 10163-4378
editor@2leafpress.org
www.2leafpress.org

2LEAF PRESS INC. is a
nonprofit 501(c)(3) organization that promotes
multicultural literature and literacy.
Stephanie Ann Agosto, Executive Director
www.2lpinc.org

Cover art: "Moonlight, Strandgade 30" by Vilhelm Hammershøi (1900-1906)
Medium: Oil on canvas
Dimensions:16 1/8 x 20 1/8 in. (41 x 51.1 cm)
Credit: Purchase, European Paintings Funds, and
Annette de la Renta Gift, 2012 (The Metropolitan Museum of Art)

Cover design: Dé-Jon Graves.
Poetry editor: Sean Dillion
Layout and design: Gabrielle David

Library of Congress Control Number: 2018951795

ISBN-13: 978-1-940939-90-2 (Paperback)
ISBN-13: 978-1-940939-91-9 (eBook)

10   9   8   7   6   5   4   3   2   1

Published in the United States of America

First Edition | First Printing

2Leaf Press trade distribution is handled by University of Chicago Press / Chicago Distribution Center (www.press.uchicago.edu) 773.702.7010. Titles are also available for corporate, premium, and special sales. Please direct inquiries to the UCP Sales Department, 773.702.7248.

"The kingdom of fairytales could be ecstasy,
but it is above all a land of pain."

—Cristina Campo

The Poems

FALLING OBJECT PROBLEMS 37

STRIP MALL 55

LEARNING TO PAINT   77

MATHEMATICS 97

Introduction to Ransom Street

I N CLAIRE MILLIKIN'S stunning new collection, *Ransom Street,* the speaker searches constantly for evidence of innocence in the world. This is a book of doubt as much as a book of hope. Loss encroaches at the end of every line to wrench hope from the speaker's mind as the "dark intersection of Persimmon and rain / awaken to morning dreams of ransom."

For Millikin, *ransom* is more than what the speaker of the book's title poem recalls as the house where "my sisters keep the secret." Ransom Street, the speaker declares, is "no house for our story." *Ransom* is more than a house or a place, however. It is "pulse, breath," dark and threatening, an empty house where the speaker has been "uninvited" and yet must inhabit.

Millikin's poems draw on the multiple meanings of *ransom* as a means of payment, deliverance, or rescue. *To be held for ransom* is to keep someone as a captive until an amount of money is paid or to try to make someone do what you want, especially by using threats. On the other hand, *to have paid a ransom* is a means of deliverance or rescue from punishment, the price for redemption. In fact, the captive is not liberated by a mere gratuitous favor, but a ransom price has been paid, for which she is set free. The original owner receives back her alienated and lost possession because she has bought it back "with a price."

The desire for redemption is at the heart of many of these poems, wherein the poet uses "my boat of language" as a means to "come back / waiting out the rest of myself." However, the arc of the book's language is combatant and works as an internal wrestling of the speaker with a panoply of family entanglements, periods in a juvenile detention center, homelessness, and abandonment.

Scattered throughout the collection, Millikin includes a series of atonement poems—both hopeful and despairing. In "Atonement: Priest," the speaker complains that "Nothing releases me; wearing even the black hat / of rain and time, as did the old priest / on Lesvos, walking an alley with grieving women, the island shining / where my mother is still a girl, pure of the knowledge of men." These lines are equal parts warning and elegy. Even so, the poem ends not with resignation but with redemption: "With each prayer, I gain back / the place before my birth, / before he touched her, and she turned."

What are these women grieving for on Lesvos? They could be mourning their widowhood, or they could be mourning the difficulties of living with men or having been accosted by the Church itself, in the guise of the priesthood. And yet, the shining island is a beacon of Lesvos, where her mother is still a girl. Also it is the Lesvos of Sappho, who celebrated erotic love and the intimate friendship between women. Thus to gain back the place *before* one's birth is to regain innocence and the pure love between mother and daughter, language and poetry.

When the speaker's mother turns around at the end of the poem, we do not know if she turns around to the priest or turns away from him. Either way, the mother is suddenly cognizant of a loss of innocence of the violent *knowledge of men* in which the victim *knows* her assailant.

And what is it the speaker gains back in returning to the island of her mother's origin? Is it the self in mourning, or is the true atonement of this poem the uncanny ability of language to heal? In one sense, the knowledge of men the mother puts on is the carnal knowledge of the Old Testament. In another sense, "to know" is the knowledge of reconnection with one's own body and voice—the final *re-at-one-ment*.

The language of the regained possession (the ransom) has been bought back with the price of redemption: the poet's acknowledgment of words to speak for the homeless, the lost, the abused and disavowed. Framing the complex relation between language, gender, and violence, Millikin's poems go out in her "boat of language / because voice is not only a wound but also a craft." ■

—Kathleen Ellis
Orono, Maine, 2018

SKELETON KEY

Atlantic

I will go out
in my boat of language
because voice is not only a wound
but also a craft.

Waves edging back and forth at the groyne,
cornerstone against erosion that itself keeps eroding.
Voice is the open place

in water, where it divides.
So also father carried us, early one morning,
a hundred miles east to the Atlantic
in a car of rust.

A piece of the sun driving toward the sun.
We crossed to the island where no one waited,
men in their boats vanishing down azimuth horizon.

On that curve of Atlantic, graveyard where ships went down
and men buried their plunder,
I thought my father was a pirate

and search all my life for what he took.
Back and forth against the groyne,
ocean wearing down the dunes.

Fishermen dropped their lines
and shadows from the pier:
ghost of road, arrow, weir,
the final slip of shelf before water takes over.

My sister turned back
but I walked the dunes' couloir,
freezing cold from a third-degree sunburn.

They wrapped me in a clean wet sheet
that night, rain driving through the verge,
awake in every nerve.

Shadowlands

From three sides of the house unfold
pinewoods, domain of feral dogs.
The sound of pines, never a human call, returns

in the city when birds' shadows
cross above lintels.
Understand there is nothing

human inside, no secret self
beyond this memory of pinewoods
where no language

spoken could leave a shadow.
Once, as children,
mother's brother walked us to the family property's edge,

pinewoods meeting train track in winter light,
branched undertow of world, beneath
taproots and bedrock, down

to the place of original thirst.
He was drunk and in earnest.
When the glass fell from the shelf,

I knelt to gather the pieces,
swept up shards and slivered glints.
The room looked empty

in its new night cleanliness.
Don't
lean against me,
I am broken.

The Year of My Death

Grandfather outlived me by five years,
collapsed at work, counting ledgers.
By then, I'd already starved, walking away
from my father, who was not his son.

Truant; walked so far into myself
I could no longer see –
something to do with B vitamin deficiency.
In exchange, got another vision, age of thirteen.

The way the ocean bends inward,
palimpsest, atomic crescendo.
Georgia elusively threads water, for rivers:
Chattahoochee, Ocmulgee, Ochlockonee, Oconee, Etowah,

all named by the Creek, who were the majority
in Georgia, until 1800. In images of black,
sepia, and silver;
the fields' far regress, those unnamed

in family photographs. Once, grandfather paid
a local historian to research his origins,
prove he was white.
In 1991, grandfather collapsed,

counting his ledgers, by which time
I'd already starved
and come back,
waiting out the rest of myself.

Quarry

The man drives his small daughters to the quarry
in afternoon light of opened granite.
Three little girls carry crayons and paper.
Almost translucent, paper when it's blank

shapes a soul. He drives the orange car.
Through open windows, sky seems to carry the riders
to quarry's jagged rock, where water rises to depth.
The sound of a stone dropped

into that water is staring down a hall into a mirror,
seeing yourself stir. Quarry fills with sequent rains,
one after the next like fate
that gathers. The father strips naked and dives

all the way down into layered water,
his body becomes shimmer, merely, shadow-cast.
Walk away, we are not made of stone
but of rain and paper and crayons

and the quarry is ours, all souls.
Naked he swims, water, pressing down and down.
Women now, my sisters sometimes telephone late at night,
speaking in voices disavowed.

Anamorphosis

Space is curved
in a house without sleep,
listening to lost
mercury dimes
rattle between floorboards
of a Depression era build-out
as trucks pass heavily down Ransom.

Space is curved at the table, where she offers
meals of winter, grit of ambivalence –
I'm still her girl;
in the pale cold mirror, my face could be hers.
Echoed feed and seed store shut dark,

curved road toward the housing projects
glistering with rain. Around the crèche
left too long after Christmas on a shelf
in someone else's mother's parlor,
space is curved.
Take also, for example, the cross-streets

between city avenues we walked at the beginning
because the car and truck motors were all going
and you touched my eyelids with your fingers,
the world curving by strings,
fluted, oscillating
luminous weight.

Orphan Afternoon

Garments do not last
unless knit of Orlon, fibers of the eternal world
spun from shale, wefted on looms of mica.
Last filling-station before pinewoods, stop here,
search the trunk for sweaters and the vagrant
tenderness of chocolate bars for supper.

That afternoon, they gave me and two other kids—
as reward for good behavior—the privilege
to ride supervised to town and purchase candy.
Just like school children—released
for an afternoon from juvenile
corrections into the eternal world.

Man in Water

On entering a hotel room, lay out hat and shoes
as if to stay for good. Light slips the winter oaks
and maybe they will forget to ask
the next payment, so you can sleep awhile.
Shirt and socks in the drawer, coat on hook.

Just before the child's birth, you used to walk the ocean's edge,
back and forth, shore flanged by forest
on both sides, waves shifting their weight.
It did not seem safe, that late fall, to walk where cars could drive.
Each afternoon, a man arrived, parked his truck in
    stony lot, stripped

off his business clothes to undershorts, dove into the Atlantic.
He'd swim the shoreline, just as you walked, back and forth,
his arms pulling through water, swimming
or praying, shoulders rising and falling.
Hard to swim the ocean; the man looked strong, folding currents.

Build a house of paper, translucent, material scar,
undone with this desire
to be innocent – to have never seen
the rivers of the Chattahoochee,
the Haw, the Eno, never to have been.

My Father's Skin

Come back to the house and he's waiting
in the backyard, wearing no shirt,
sunlight tight on his neck and shoulders,
oak branch shadows veining his skin.

For years, the damages held invisible
the way memory waits under the surface.
In time, sun's marks turn dangerous,
but in childhood, that's all there is: heat on cells.

In the backyard chair he reads Milton; the garden's defunct,
as if someone hard purposely emptied the earth,
but it was only us to ourselves.
Seeds rapid and tough, without translation, sunk into red dirt.

His skin later had to be removed, in small harmed places
as can never be done with memory, breath, and pulse.
My father says it's time. Come in
to the empty house.

Shadows with their tendons of breath
hold the inherited light. Keeping
all this in mind, I avoid the sun—
not to get in the car, not
to ride with him this time.

As Snow Closes in the City

She is reading a story aloud in the bar
and you're sure you've heard it before.
Snow closing the ways between buildings,
alleys, inlets, quays to harbor.

She is reading a story you already remember,
the language prehensile,
what gets taken.
In the restrooms, they are servicing men,

but you'll walk away now,
snow shutting its sliding milk.
This mother tongue,
a language to stutter and earn.

It's always over and begins again, snow masting
skies of open doors.
Shed the scanty dress of the delinquent
off the shoulder of time.

Dress of a Thousand Petals

Ancestors shape a shadow tree, no one can say
what happened to them, how desperate they became
to arrive at being echo only.
I could no longer bear to come home as a beggar

the way trees lose their leaves, done with sunlight
that has gone too far into them, turned
wrists' pulse of ransom.
In childhood, we traveled without destination,

quick, toward the edge—
which city, which bed. Without house,
men found me early, an easy mark.
I've lived in this town before,

its streets of erased trees—Oak, Poplar, Mulberry—
toponymy. At the dark intersection
of Persimmon and rain, I awaken
to morning dreams of ransom.

Ransom Street

A street I already remember:
each night sweep from the room
the thousand petals of sun

sepal, whorl, alate blossoms into street.
This sleeplessness by which I pay
for the stillness of evening.

He says the room is clean, the oaks
ghosts in their own right,
never lie about it;

but my sisters keep the secret.
Ransom extends down
hill, straight through the town,

pulse, breath,
no other world returns,
no house for our story.

Nostalgia

The bloodstain on the sheet is mine,
though I'd pretend otherwise. This is home.

The basement apartment's no longer rented out.
A bright sky masks the yard.

If there in the narrow front road, I could divest myself, move on.
But doves, with their voices of doors,

call back, hallways opening to further night.
I swear, this is the last time for this place.

Unearthly shimmer of doves' chirr.
But it's never cold enough, and I'll return

to the same hallway where I first learned to run;
that speed my lexicon

of heaven, grift of earth,
foot-strikes echoing, night —

dark glass, reflecting down Ransom.

A Musical Gift

The first instruments were flutes
of bone, stick, breath.

Mother played baroque
emotions, but I never mastered

any instrument except voice,
chanting Orthros in the winter church

when no one's in the congregation.
Just the priest, aching for the Lord indivisible.

Voice goes inside
marrow. It's the same

when photographs carry childhood
as shadow to solid.

The rooms of performance smell faintly of solvents.
They stand

a long way from the unhealed place of music.

Martin Heidegger's Taxi Service

He drives the taxi to my uncles' farm,
and I am telling you it arrives.
It arrives and Heidegger stole everything
from Hölderlin, who could not save himself.
Try again, for the world is at hand.

But I write these words in my own hand:
do not trust the sun, waiting tables also
will destroy your trust in men.
They stand so close,
their shadows slant your pulse.

No other hallway to cross, get past it,
between mother's brothers' farms,
a boundary: the fields'
deep pale frame of light, elusions.
Heidegger, who cheated Hölderlin, drives

the taxi in stiff rain, crossing
to the open place;
because the ones who are sacrificed sometimes
get a second voice. The sacrificed
sometimes get a second voice:

Hölderlin survived
years in captivity, writing translations
into his own made-up language,
Pallakis, pallasch, my beloved.

The Structure of Boxes

As night is shaped of boxes, (Archimedean squares),
my grandfather built flimsy houses.
The nature of boxes is to be built of sky,
a supply from which my grandfather drew indiscriminately
so that now, in bad dreams, I am folding

the house of last equations,
early transcendental functions
carrying the line. Stand at the bus stop in rain,
almost starving, watching
a petrel rise in a box of sky.

The nature of boxes: symmetry,
structured as they are of sequential, hinged squares.
It comes down to the reason
I waited at the bus stop, the reason to starve
rather than accept his offer.

My father translated his body to sky
and I got blamed for the fall-out,
rain in my mouth.

Even now, I speak that language of the unsealed box,
open and shut, a box
cannot be broken for horizon
goes all the way back.

Cranes

Deeper into houses, what use for keys?
As houses multiply, fields die down, fold
also tobacco warehouses
stained by bright leaf.

Cranes pass at night into winter,
in their sky above scars, a thrown history:

City of cranes; this always
empty house where I find you,
undone by that illness of which we say nothing,
nothing more to be done.

So uninvited have I been,
only you always letting me in.
The city of our birth turns mercury bright,
new construction shimmering like Christmas.

All night buses pass behind trees,
shopping malls, warehouses,
and the wealthy stay wealthy.
Cranes of folded paper thrown to sky.

Canned Goods

Grandmother removes from evening's cupboard
canned goods to fill us
with lead solder and salt
at the scarred elm table.

It rains off and on, slow flicker
at the junction between towns;
sometimes, the cars
of the wealthy break down.

Once, grandmother took me to ride with her
through the carwash, water falling across us –
ablution, a fine mineral milk.
On the other side, we came through

to a day of clear glass.
So that when he took me to the apartment of his ex,
she saw I was not much more than a child
and said nothing to protect me.

The city was dark
and bright, like a coloring book
of lines filled in carefully
and with too much force.

Skeleton Key

Even the child digging in dirt
can come home now,
turn the key he finds in earth,
unlock the house.

My sisters and I were trained at piano,
the damaged inroads of winter. Taking lessons
primed us for a certain kind of suffering:
to be told what to do,
his hands on your hands.

At the corner of the room, birds' shadows
vanish into winter. Migratory
key, undertow music
that shifts when interpreted.

Never speak aloud –
grandmother warned – your dreams
until after breakfast,
until they are only messages.

Fish House

Grandfather taught us to fish the spring before
I turned ten. Rain cast its lines into lake,
fish rising to the mirror lure,
mouthing all the way
to the oak slab where grandfather gutted them.
The blood of the fish is not language,
but it leaves a mark.

In bad dreams, I am still cleaning floors for a living,
a skill at which I so excelled, that by the end,
I could erase the tracks of anything –
animal, human, divine –
of water, air, or earth.

A book is ephemeral, built of names or numbers.

Madonna

Left in the closet, old-style tennis shoes
with soles worn off at the heels
as if she were dragging herself through it, every step.

I have almost written the book of lost objects:
stray birds hinge upon it (crane,
anhinga, skua, cormorant).

Fishing for dimes at the gas station pay-phone
before town cedes to salt marsh,
in her dove gray gloves –

I fill the tank because we have a long way to drive
easterly, sky's picking up salt.
After eviction,

it's over; all but the gas station ledgers at a fold
of light. All night, I watched her
reflected in the window glass, holding the infant

boy in her lap; back and back through dark windows
ran the image so that time
might never erase.

Go

Played Go in the cold kitchen all that last winter
Leaden paint was legal, grandfathered in.

The point of the game is closing distances.
Even at smallest angles, winter
intends the gaps
beyond trees.

When it's over, it's over:
he leaves, he's no longer yours.
Wires inside walls, (veins)
brought light, (vision)
pertaining only to that house.

The sound from the forest
sometime resembled fire,
but it was just winter sky, nothing burning,
sticks of trees in wind.

We played Go because the game is complex
enough to make you forget, while you play it,
hunger and cold. You can play through
scant rented house, wearing wool hats

indoors to stay warm. Nothing within belonged to us
except the photographs of his natural daughter
stowed beneath the bed with old sweaters
worn at elbows, awaiting patches.

The Rain Thieves

What they take away is not immediately apparent.
Known only by its absence,
wells tightening in dry summer.

Schooled as we were for silence,
my sisters and I have gotten nowhere.
We hand away our similes unthinkingly,
for the rain thieves are interested in daughters.

What they steal cannot be seen,
its loss leaves nothing.
Behind grandfather's sold house,

pomegranate, persimmon,
kinglets, and doves.
I cannot tell the story of how it happened
because it happened in heavy rain, a closed door.

He says, *come kneel down,* help me,
and I am still digging
for the names of the dead and the living,
the burned collars of roses.

Frozen Food

Stock frozen food, how else
to carry winter inland and weep

without speaking of the reason?
Frozen food, immemorial, keep

that taste when evening leans so near
you can't bear to see it.

Your brother-in-law will drive you home afterwards, saying,
be quiet about it.

Ice shapes the garden to its kind
because ice pressed close

against any other substance,
held long enough, makes all ice.

Open and shut, the small places of survival,
the little stories you might tell.

FALLING OBJECT PROBLEMS

Falling Object Problems

To tell the path by which an object falls,
pay attention to the room where it slipped.
An object dropped will fall at the rate of gravity,
a zero that holds the world.

Maybe the object falling describes the path
to a house in the American Midwest where you'll rent
from a woman who offers one set of clean sheets
and, for your infant, the toys her daughter left.

The initial velocity of falling is zero,
leading you to believe in the possibility of survival,
but the object accelerates at a fixed rate
and you have to live with the consequences.

Gravity in the shelter of Church and Howe,
shivering, starved down 'til you fit
a shale town in the Midwest. Stay here, stay
folding the stained pajamas she gives you for the child.

The path by which objects fall
can be charted by equations
that never give the reason –
for the fall itself, nor dropped versus thrown.

Equations for a falling body never solve
without variables. It takes time to fall,
but once the fall begins, the course
of the object rarely changes, just the skin

of sky's drag. I thought I'd find a way back east,
but the language of gravity lays a stone on the tongue.
Hold on,
this shell game of missing forces,

milk of snow and red birds' open voices.
Nothing falls now. It is winter in the house.

Interlocutor

As a young child, I'd ask my mother
questions to which I already knew the answer,
Obvious questions—Who was the first
President of America? Which is more
money, a nickel or a dime? I wanted only
to hear her voice, that I loved.
But she thought I was quizzing her,
and grew angry, *What a hard girl you are,*
showing off how you know the answers.

We are driving still, in my mind, past the bank
to the post office to mail a letter
to her mother, and I am the small daughter
in the back seat, asking *What is the name*
for grandmother in French?
Dusk draws its burgundy line
across the town, tense and infinite.

Dead letter-office,
who will long for my voice
enough to make up questions
without answers—dusk light folds up the sky
through windows, oak and hickory. Night's

letter might still arrive
for my daughter without a name.

Pretty Dresses

Gas pumps by a dark field,
live oaks, and the night
jars circle. Little hawks of the inland mind.

Cotton fields give no protection from night's distance,
or from bad dreams, when I'm backed against a cinderblock wall.

Traveling back roads into Georgia, we'd stop
where no one much lived, gas pumps by cinderblock
and cotton fields, me wearing grandfather's jacket from the war.

Girl Jumping Rope

The circling rope rhymes
her heart's anorexic clock,
then the screech of backyard peacocks
in a sudden fall of snow.

She keeps the rope's tempo, ellipse
under attic's ceiling arc. Plastic
Christmas tree in the corner
casts aciculate shadow,

as in a winter forest. Below,
a kitchen painted deepest blue,
a woman stitching salt into the soup.
The girl jumps through an empty rope,

a bent zero. Beneath her,
the neighborhood disappears,
forfeit into ashen snow. Even those
guarded by the dog
did not survive Pompeii.

Suitcase Philosophy

My childhood of suitcases unfolded
in other countries; I'd come home
to a house mostly empty,
cinderblock structure by the river.

L'Hopital's rule tells you
what to do when confronted by zero
divided by zero: a suitcase
without a house for return.

After thunderstorm and hail,
this swept emptiness of survival
houses built on the hillside
for last century's wealthy—fall apart now.

Painted pink and virid green,
watching the mountain,
dissolute flaking lead paint:
home is elsewhere. For catechism,

learn this vagrancy, this living on.
It will be evening before supper,
a long edge to hunger.
Empty your suitcase, it's done.

Rice Fields Shadows

Hallways rice-colored in late afternoon light,
the sky makes of doorways shadows.

Run faster and there will be no house.
I know that my soul is a hole
in the shape of the visible world.

Not to speak of it, to not lay down
this dark work I do.

Chalk Music

Someone's child drew on sidewalks
chimeras of purple and green, ephemera
lasting only 'til it rained.
For a while, I found my way by them:
by the music from the opposite apartment,

Armenian or Greek, through open windows.
The notes threw the sky forward,
freakish clarity of early spring light
where shadows cross the line
from dirt to concrete.

That music of pure intention,
in the high notes the singer's distance
from sky touches skin. All things will disappear,
sunlight moving into the grass
by small, ineluctable divisions.
So memorize the details,

invoke this chalk music for my absolution
when nothing's left after spring rain.

Cloth Mother

I descend from a long line of failed mothers.
Mostly, it was no one's fault –
they died giving birth, or just after.
And yet, my own mother survived,

only half listening as I tried
new words, stylus,
to call her back
rocks and stones and trees.

I descend from a line of women
whose dresses were preserved, polyester, silk,
in mirrored closets. Early
I knelt to touch the garments

that smelled of sweat and fear, *earth's
diurnal course.* In the attic, two rooms back,
dresses from two centuries earlier.
Put on the dresses of ghosts, sure, but take them off

before that fate catches you also, little bird.
Cloth is a curious substance:

cousin of breath, but heavier. Rented
that place above a pizza shop in New Haven,

walked downstairs for free coffee tasting of sausage,
and the men cooing *little one, little one.*
From the sill, the doves' small shadows curved,
almost and never human.

Hands' Shadows

Between a hand and its shadow,
bad dreams of inheritance. I slept
on a mattress taken from the bed
of a friend's truck—free gift
of rust, rain, sky,
what the truck had carried
as it crossed east toward New Haven.

Don't think about it, succor, haven
what could be sanctuary. As a child,

I believed animals could speak, if only
someone found the proper way to translate.
I gathered my father's typing paper,
spread it like shale in the yard,
poured paint in bowls at the paper's edge, and culled
the neighborhood pets to walk through.

In the footprints of dogs and cats, a language
I tried to translate, quick and desolate,
but it walked away from me into the forest.

The shadows of hands, a way of speaking, what else?
When we first married, we bought a mattress,
clean and unused,
but I was already worn out
from the places I'd traveled through.

The Movie Houses

i

A capital, a language, what persists.
The sound of rain is the sound of objects
rain touches, audible shapes. The sound of words
is the sound of objects language touches,
a forest translated. And I could weep for it,
the cold clean place.

ii

She found me thumbing by the grassy median, offered a ride,
that her home become mine.
But I loved the movie house instead:
images, language, rain sounding
along the back doors and the alley behind.

iii

Winter coming into wrists and cheekbones;
as I went deeper toward the screen,
a forest, a cloth of words appeared.
Each day, I walked the aisles, found my seat
deeper in, so she could no longer claim me.

iv

To recover a language takes patience, depth, calculus,
confocal lines. I will speak of ideas, not emotions,
because the movies run
so close my skin.

Cinemas of Tifton, Georgia

At the field's edge, Aunt called in the horse, holding
in the flat of her hand a small apple. The animal
almost knelt, dipping its head, dark
curve of sky's evening. But I am confusing

the storyline. All this happened
before I was born. Before her daughter
was killed. I only remember hearing the story, not seeing the field
where my aunt, who once was beautiful, turned.
She could not bear what happened
and stopped bathing, brushing her teeth, matted
hair like a saint's. They ate from her hands, I'm told.

For each new year, I cut open
a pomegranate, feeding the seeds to my son. Some I eat myself
because blood is blood.

Old Devil's Step

i

A few scant leaves of trash, Christmas
wrapping papers fallen into the road,

at dawn, animals fighting awaken you,
cry open a place where human words do not fit.

ii

The faces of ancestors get lost in photographs
that never show the back of time,
thin-walled house in winter—

armies once bivouacked in the yard here,
leaving red dirt irons from their tents.
Open eyes of the wounded traced this night.

iii

Thin walls shake as night trains pass
through their skin of exhaustion.
The first owner worked the defunct mill;

on the street, dogs are fighting
for a hard terrain. Transcendence
is only a matter of staying awake
for days on end in winter, listening.

STRIP MALL

Intersection

Against the counter-rhythm of the train behind the trees,
pinewoods are waiting for something,
a winter table set with milk,
transubstantial between branches—

my sisters and I, swaying with the men
at the corner smoking
before the age of reason.

Milk

They left us alone in other countries, pressed
to so many languages, our words
became myriad,
image on image, palimpsest.

These winter mornings, I run Ransom,
slope of half-paved hill. Beyond that,
pinewoods, train-line
with its sound of wound,
a plant firing coal, smoke
from its tower
sifting down like milk.

Strip Mall

Walk the parking lot at night
until the space feels endless,
your parents circling in their car of ashes.

In this last tenancy,
animals of the nearby zoo bend in their stalls
and snow turns inland. Come closer, it will be your miracle.

The dress of a thousand petals
is written in such rooms, just as you fear: unprotected
by thin doors into storm.

Zoos, parking lots,
and tobacco fields
were invented in America.

Coat History

He gives up his coat to subsidize winter
in the late afternoon hotel,
puts the coat on my shoulders,
and the jobs he has lost, one after the other,
do not matter when held against winter's touch.

The substance of a coat covers the body:
cousin of paint on wall, soldier's maille.
In its heart,
a coat shapes a dark corner
where you are an animal, afraid.

When I walked out to fenced cattle, one cow leaned toward me,
lowered her head, and muzzled the coat I wore all winter
that had been his grandfather's,
a thin man. So the coat fit
a half-starved girl. Inside a coat, history

of every lost wearer. We must put them on, no safety
in nakedness, however incandescent
light shines through thinned fabric.
The coat, from kneeling, gets worn at the knees;

say that prayer again, the human one. The cow's tongue
traveled rough wool to my neck,
and then I turned, like a child from its mother
done with love.

Snake Handlers

Foot-washing Baptists
took my name for daughter, enraptured
with how I could memorize scripture
as if it were written in me. Light
burns through leaves,
oak and maple down to nothing, spent

nous when wind takes branch shadows
and makes them vanish
into girls and men.
For the snake is not king,
but watches, coral, rattle, copper
hard glister of its names.

Saint Lucy

When men cut out her eyes, Saint Lucy
became blind. Or enlightened,
depending on interpretation.

A friend, who took me to live with her at thirteen,
understood the nature of my unseeing;
her seven older brothers waited also
in the bright and shadowed upstairs hall.

Traveling by car, you lose yourself.
So I never became a driver.

Lucy's eyes filled with the holy-spirit: hence
her eyes were taken during torture
and God replaced them
with bright stones.

A stony distance opens,
having once been filled
with too much sight.

Holy, Unholy

A word says most at its breaking point,
like trees in high winds. How you hear their structure
only when sky presses that far;

after ballet, I'd wait for the bus to take me home
where mother was sleeping,
the metal breadbox empty, disavowed
coats and shoes of men. I open the door,

taking their hats and coats, brush the leaves,
haulm, broken pieces of sky. The sound of the trees
is the sound of sky finding
words that can be broken.

Or sometimes, something holds the form intact.
Auctoris anima ad dominum—
He recalls nothing
for which to ask forgiveness—
this coat he puts on in dreams,

so early morning I wake up
searching the torn pockets.

Sky Clothes

At each airport, buy new clothes
and the sky will forget you.

A clean wound heals completely. So, erase yourself.
Who flies free these days?

The reasons for travel grow cold,
carrying the same suitcase

in and out of this world.
And your father will meet you at the gate

late night in Carolina. The sky warm as mercury,
he will take your bag on his shoulder

and you can eat, a few bites now, from the apple
after the long journey

without fearing what it will cost.
The wounds on the Cross were five,

healed angelically by the vanishing body, transitus.
At each station, buy new clothes,

cover your hands and feet,
leaving open the slit of your dress

for your father's hand to reach.
Because your son won't hear the story

from you. He'll only inherit
sky clothes you bought, immaculate garments:

four times the nail, once the sword.
Edge without world.

When I Got Religion

Sleep-dark water in which I swam,
my father watching my shoulders for a woman's.
After that submersion, never breathe the same or rise again,
nouns for baptism
say the words:
or nothing,
a breach of shoulders, sun
dividing the trees into cries.
I have wasted my time.

In middle school, I was already that girl
who looks like a woman, but I shut it down fast,
fasting until the flesh vanished,
light on stripped winter branches.

Maybe winter is not yet over,
maybe I yet will be invited
into the house of a girl my age
with seven older brothers
to be fed rice cooked by her sorrowful mother,

who will not become anything now
but a mother of sons.
A late freeze comes down hard,
killing after spring's premorse thaw.

After the Garden of Forking Paths

Drive past the Inn-Town apartments
where I lived as an infant; in a small room of heaven, perhaps.
Daughters can be dangerously misnamed –
fulmar, skua, petrel, plover;
from the shore, they disappear.

To find the way of it, start over. Down the road,
a power station burns coal, fly-ash, slag.
Body of Christ, bread of salvation,

this darkening lease, narrow rooms
in which mother sang in her mother tongue,
the language that will slowly tear me apart
and thereby enter the world.

The holy place is a few words
about nowhere to buy good food,
just junk for the motherless,
someone kneeling for it.

Hallways

Always an ending and a beginning,
a hallway closes and opens.
But I want only a way home where on the hook,
grandfather's coat waits delicate and bereft,

a slender man who fought in mid-century wars.
On the glassed porch, the night-
blooming cereus opens, vulnerable as a hand.
Turn it on, he says, *it should be yours—*

this radio he cobbled together from wire
as a ten-year-old boy attuned to the distances,
sublunary hallways
from which the house extends

into highways, ash trees, interstellar sky.
A slender soldier, he fought on that beach,
feet in the corridor of water
as men crossed over.

When I was Blonde

My hair was blond when I was born;
father put his hand on my golden head.

It will rain soon and she's raking the walk, incautious
of the rough sky and tall oaks.

I cannot remember what that way took,
to be golden. Sky weighs heavier than light,

molecules of water and dirt, earth, eluvium
fly through us, breath by breath.

He opened his palm on my golden head.
Mother, sleeping in her corner realm, said nothing.

So I caught words from the neighbors,
ex-patriots like us, from somewhere else.

Mandarin was my first language.
Now that translation hurts like spilled weather.

It falls into the room through the radio
towers of dark oaks, flickering gold.

I could not lie in that language
that my mother never taught me,

that my father did not understand.
Gold light just before night, she says all I have asked

has only upset you, this history.
As it happened, my hair in grade school grew dark and pure,

the kind that touches night.
The radio plays a scalene mirror.

Was it his touch or something in me, uneasy,
the feet of Christ walking
a perpendicular sky.

Second Hallway

In Sunday school, I was the smartest girl; but I got lost
in the Lord's battle with time, an untranslated house.
A hallway can be an escape route,
doorways structure its mind.

Winter in his father's house that night;
I awoke, walked down the hall, and saw in the mirror
(that ended the hall my never born daughter) untranslatable,
a stir of light in wrists, fractal haul

waiting at the bus station when a man drives up, *come on,*
his face blurred with longing. In the Lord's battle with time,
light is fire: needed and dangerous. We rode a long way in his car,
the highway a hallway
seven days deep.

The Robe

They gave me a robe:
stripes straight down, cotton-polyester blend.
Secretly, I loved the pattern:
the way it fit my small hips, making me an arrow

to fly. Fletcher, I tied the robe tight—
to be human again, hear voices
in the hallway, slow stems of rain
across pinewoods, anything.

How delicate the weft of solitary confinement.
When I got out, I could not speak of it.
The mathematics teacher promised me, *If you say nothing,*
all that has happened will disappear, as no man will care
because you'd still be a beautiful girl,

if you'd just wear some make-up. A girl can be anything,
pinewoods proved under their garments of rain,
robe of contemplation. Jesus also waited
in his celled transfiguration,
a stutter at the marrow of the human.

The robe so nearly my own, bereft
when I got out,
as in movies when men and women fall
out of love.

Table Laid for an Evening Meal

Men play chess at evening, back and forth
across stone tables in the park.
They could be statues, almost,
for their silence and stillness. But the games are real.

Pawn myself bit by bit; the rook cheats space
less than the angled bishop, in shadowed slant
of branches, because here was once forest,
night folding at its hook.

Retreat, begin again;
at evening, when nowhere is home,
open spaces between buildings grow luminous.
The men in the park play chess, calm and fierce,

as if it mattered. Hands on the pieces like prayer.
Only this tactic of chance,
for the darkness of my shoes,
the places I keep walking.

In my pockets,
I stow nothing, nothing at all.
Only my eyes carry this late sky
game of strategy.

Musical Chairs

Musical chairs is a zero sum game: children circle
an ellipse of chairs as music plays,
and a teacher quietly pulls away
one chair per round, then stops
the music so that one child falls into empty space.

Those children listening too closely, caught by song,
lose out, not watching as the teacher snatches
their intended nest.
The winners never look away.

I fell gracefully. For many years,
this was my best gift: being small and deft,
well-versed in catching myself.
Was it worth it—
to pay no attention to the game,
just hear the music all the way through, inside

lips, eyes, wrists, down to the place of pulse?
Chrysostom, dark gold chrysalis, falling
when teacher pulls my soul;
chimera, a falling body

also rises. Remember
the bodiless captains of angels—
music of state fair carousel,
celestial spheres.

LEARNING TO PAINT

Caesura

In the car, she turns to face me, idling at the train crossing.
I've been a high school student for ten days, autumn writes
its fault lines though branches, along the tracks.

Sun's needle always leads back
into the veins of pines and hematite.
A house without furniture

remembers the sky best—
sunlight, brilliant on the dash.
Without a door, so holy the sky;

home from juvenile corrections for ten days, dry
annealed sunlight
glazes the windshield. She stares,

accusing me without saying. So I'm opening the door,
taking up my long walking away,
wearing my dress of wax.

The Summer I
Learned to Paint

I was terrible at the part of painting that involves patience.
Watch the trees shift in wind, it happens so quickly.
If you look too long, the movement's indistinct,
as in slow shutter speed photographs.

All summer, I lived in the attic apartment
of a half-abandoned Victorian taken up
by girls who worked the stables past New Haven.
Sundays, they returned, reeking and expiated.

I studied painting on my day off
from washing laundry, at which I excelled:
I can clean any stain, even the cloth
of Veronica, sudarium, sweating with the effort.

The painting instructor got furious at me.

All that talent, and for what purpose?
But this world is not translation
It is itself the mirror, light without voice.

It took a long time for the face to emerge,
stained by anguish. Stand quiet,
memorize the texture
of light, supernumerary damages.

She'd say slow down, patience,
but too late. I'd already gotten caught
speeding seventy miles per hour over the limit,
and all the rest is waiting it out.

Gray Eyes Once Were
Believed To See Ghosts

Riding the train wearing my mother's blue shoes,
wind tearing off pieces of trees –
these shoes first belonged to her mother –
I am stepping the paths of ghosts.

Time Swallowed by Light

Rough luggage of time;
in the apartment, we had almost no furniture, only light
that swallows all things and time eating the light,
filling the shallow stairwell,

tannic veins of autumn; when we come home,
red earth swept dry before the open door,
tracked in by our shoes
carries the field.

Solitary

Turning fifteen in solitary,
I wrote a letter to my grandmother
asking that her name be returned to me, atonement

in the narrow room where rain cast its shadow sideways,
nothing else, a high window, cut of sky.
Grandmother wrote back with thread and needle,
sending a dress
to wear once I got out.

I asked for her to return my name,
and she gave me such clothes
as done leaves are made of,
fire, fragile gold.

Do not watch,
she is turning the leaves under her heart,
namesake.

Taxi-cab

Taxi takes me late through temporary stays,
down the grift of what vanishes.

Wood-cutters at the side of the road, leaning
all the way into Warren County,
north through Aroostook.

There is no destination.
The driver's right-hand drifting to my wrist
braced on the dash.

Late at night, on the tongue, the sweetness
of rain's rising and falling, sibilant.
A hole in the night, around which the taxi circles.

The dead remain, not an invention of time,
but its extension.
He says—*I saw you. I swore to the other cab drivers*
I would be the one to drive you.

Atonement: Plastic

Even so, you will be broken with longing
for the plastic Christmas tree your parents purchased
the one year they tried to have the holiday at home.

A distance to drive
back the street in rain:
generations vanish, names become moths,
but the psaltery of plastic stays.
The patience of plastic is almost everlasting.
Plastic are the words on the table, the open book.

Contingent on recitation, the psalm.
Contingent on mirrors, the body.
Contingent on breath, blood.

Laky

The hardest red,
water stacked deep above clay bed.
Cast in the line. What is animated,
what has soul, is the lake itself.

While other teenage girls grew strong,
I fasted. My bones grew hollow.
Flight depended on that lightness, ascesis,
open the golden marrow,
fish caught in winter's husk.

Hotel Room Atonement

I never tell anyone about my father, a limit
where the photograph folds
toward God. In backyard super 8,
my baby sister dances naked,
wet leaves stick to her skin.

I never tell the truth about myself; thus,
in bad dreams, the stone cutters by the highway
turn their heads
and the old women say,
it was bound to happen.

Atonement: Pinewoods

Deeper in, birds get so quick
you cannot tell the difference
between a bird and shadow, fugitive,

and your grandparents will no longer
be taking you for a late supper
at the Quik Mart on the corner, so folded
in earth as they are now.

That bird has flown.

Key Left in Pocket

The red river moves

back and forth. I finger my lost and found key,
haptic distance, sanctuary,
a jagged exact psalm—
set for a lost house

useless, and intact.
After the war, grandfather brought home
this jacket he would not put on,
and could not give away. I inherited it.

In the cold pocket of the river, Orpheus
stammered and it was raining
in grandfather's coat.
Key left in pocket, rub palm

and finger to serrated edges,
so precise a hasp, that last voice,
key left in the pocket
of a jacket that no longer fits.

Parking Lots at Night

In the movie theater, father's mother waits;
gloves in her lap, her pale coat folded
in the customary back row. Stop trying.
Watch the movie, go back down

where your heart is pure
of time. River of vision, always double,
the movies run, two for one —

bite the ticket on your tongue,
theater, lyric scar.

Back Kitchen

Long dormant, childhood's utensils wait
in their places to be conjured: battered
whisks and spatulas, dented aluminum pots;

here she'd stir tomatoes, her sauce taking on
such metallic taste. I'd know it still
for the lost gloss of evening.

Ill-kept house, but the sky goes inside
and covers the table.
As I was driving home almost a ghost,

hands tight on the wheel, watching the rearview,
live oak cut by sky. Take away
green shoots, leaving only outline.

The forest of the kitchen is stark.
A few spices she kept, pepper, paprika, and salt
from the year of my birth. She hated to cook,

fed us our own hunger.
The door to her bedroom cracked,
she weeps or dreams rough.

Set up the stuff of supper, viaticum:
draw water at the stiff tap,
open the rice box left over

from the last visit, an earlier husband.
Sweep from the counter crumbs
of shadow. This is my kitchen now.

Atonement, Mirror

If we walk into the house,
none will await us but ancestors
offering soup thick with salt.
They will speak our names for thirst.

Arcades of oak trees fold away
into vespers' dark box of leaves.
When my baby sister and I collided,
running at a game of tag, my teeth
kissed her forehead hard,

printing a star
for which I cannot atone.
No wonder it has happened.
I've ended up with any man, trying
to get the rain out of my shoulders.

MATHEMATICS

Make-Up Tips From Juvie

That autumn just before release,
harvest tugging at wheat,
the older girls gave me make-up tips—
so that in high school I'd look clean—

across my skin drew their hands, hid the months
spent in solitary with tanning foundation,
smoothed suffering from my eyes, kohl
to open the frame of sight.

Red leaves shake down that straight sky.
Time to return to school.

Imagine the point becomes a line, a square, a cube,
a fourth dimension: rain through rain in a cold house.

That autumn they taught me to wear make-up.
For the beauty of empty fields does not kneel, but unfolds.

Maybe I have nothing left
but this story.

Atonement: Priest

I touch the bread that becomes flesh
and dream at night of drowning; of fish in my hands,
useless for protection against the ocean's depths.

Nothing releases me; wearing even the black hat
of rain and time, as did the old priest
on Lesvos, walking an alley with grieving women, the island
shining
where my mother is still a girl, pure of the knowledge of men.

With each prayer, I gain back
the place before my birth,
before he touched her, and she turned.

Night: Here

Close the doors,
the shadow painting torn from the trees
enters the house.

A baby is crying at night, but the baby isn't yours.
A woman in heels crosses the parking lot
between roses, doorways, and the planetarium:

she is your mother, but you're never her concern.
Close the doors, night now.
The painting torn from the trees

moves by shadow against the walls,
tree roots mirrored in branches,
shadow of buried form

tied to night as rain carries thirst.
Never her concern,
a wet parking lot, heavy with the broken scent

of autumn roses. What's done is done.
Night, not immaterial, but of the farthest medium;
not immaterial, no, but intangible.

You will never be an apprentice.
Always, you will know too much to begin;
boys will already have taken you to their rooms,

closed the doors at night.
Maybe she never claimed you,
but you have inherited her slender ankles and fugitive step.

Night tears the trees' shadow-paintings from their skin,
sway along the walls, immersion.
Say yes, say the synod of angels

passes, *yes*
the hallway's caught in darkness,
so you cannot see.

Keeping House

Shadows you cannot save, too fragile,
bent beneath sun. And uncle's dancing
because now he has the money.

Even so, this house must be kept secret;
to be safe, code everything

of that tongue borrowed down – cheat if you must.
Then at the last, tell the truth. All of it.

Seattle's Daughter

Your soul stuck to the glass plate
when the man with a dark box
forced your photograph, named you Princess Angeline.
These days, I must peel it free;
the process is painful, like any answering.

You alone stayed on the shore, Seattle's daughter,
the others forced off, and many died of the wound.
But you persisted
where you were born.
A sky of lead settled on your tongue

when they would not listen as you spoke,
your inherited language.
But you refused
to learn another lexicon.

White children threw stones at you as you hung
the clothes you washed for their mothers.

Tight the path to your most narrow house.
I drove there once, by accident, to Seattle,
all the way from western Georgia, Muscogee County,
in the blue car of an early failed marriage.
Used to think I'd get by on my strength alone.

Unmake the false name, *Princess Angeline.*
I drove to your coast for nothing
but a room in a gray house I could not own
and the dream of a coat—you know that dream—
a coat with a map of the heavens
stitched inside, star by star,
Seattle's eldest daughter.

The Apartments of Displaced Persons

She visits, bringing late night's hunger,
saying you must learn to cook
before low blood sugar hits, sinking
down the vein. She lays down
rugs carried from her parents' country.

She vows to stay and teach
until you have mastered her recipes—
all that she wrote
of hunger, untranslated, unappeased.

Cold House

To save money, he kept the house cold.
In winter, we wore hats, coats, gloves
around the supper table at dusk.

The way a word encloses a hand
my father would say, *open the door,*
and the cold night entered us.

Take branches of longleaf pine and stripped live-oak,
start a fire for warmth without a hearth.
This duration, this living-through.

Leaving the Party

Katadesmoi, words for the dead from the living:

leave by the back porch, where father's shoes waiting
before the door signify
this is a house of drowning;

walk barefoot past willows' curve,
mother waking at evening
to burn our supper and weep.

Piano Lessons

I am a ruined person,
but I know how to play the piano:
they put me in a room to play the instrument.
I thought, there are other things

that I do better than playing the piano.
But nothing else was in the room
except a piano, set by a window,
the sash flaking lead paint.

Down the hill, houses darkened,
framed in the gray window.
In the room I played piano, light slipping
into the veins of sky, a fiery map at evening.

In other houses, men were celebrated
for copying the symmetry that I created.
Eventually, lead-dust and winter
will converge,

arrive at the same place,
the instrument by an open window,
pith of the house,
a room that cannot be healed.

Cardboard Houses

I got a cardboard house, for Christmas,
age eight. A photograph
left in a shoebox proves it:
my cardboard house, built in the hallway

between foyer and formal dining parlor.
The cardboard house shaped a hollow
high and wide enough for a child
of forty pounds and forty-eight inches.

Cardboard house painted and squared
to mimic Georgian architecture,
charmed the slanted light of hallway.
So long I have skirted fate,

my cardboard house. But I always knew
hunger for a story in the blood
the way the leaves at autumn's edge catch
fire: some stranger, farther light

for witness, and women like me, often enough,
end up in cardboard houses, sleeping rough.

Atone

Because my mother was beautiful,
I have a hard time letting go.

At evening, we sit at the table.
Trees slate the house with shadows.

The trees are blue
and the quickness of autumn vanishes into them.

A voice turns inward;
after all, it cannot be helped.

Between the stripped
branches of oak, small snow

on the table of earth, eluvium, transient silt.
We are waiting, our feet on thin soil,

to pull a meal from blue cupboards,
plates set for atonement. Fire's flute

to ashes, she douses
her cigarette before walking out.

The Abandoned

Down 8th street to the east, stores shut in heavy rain,
so we'll have nothing to eat at evening.

My grandparents lived above a hairdresser shop
an hour west of Alma, Georgia: two rooms,
the walls of the kitchen painted black
for elegance and cleanliness,
never to show the singe.

In the space between dreams and breath,
abandoned now that building of red brick,
with rows of bulbous hairdryers
echoing in stained mirrors
on the street-level floor.

Darts

Once was an ace at darts, held
between loves,
skill to strike the heart,

that vulnerable circle
where fate holds still. Easy
one staring winter

to hit the bull's eye,
pull the soul, red exergue.
Striking, I'd hear a sigh

just audible, and any man would touch my wrist,
a dark room behind the light
in which to dance, throw my weight.

The trick is not to try,
steady thumb and eye, and think
away yourself.

That winter of little to eat, I threw darts straight
before a darkened mirror,
reflection pinned

with narrow, winged stings.
An ace, just for a season that didn't last,
in winter, when it mattered least;

I won at games played in smudged light,
stars burning themselves out
by analog distance.

Back Story

A house happens twice:
where I am broken,
where I survive.

Where my father works into the night
(for night is his life's work),
Where he turns on the television,

its flat blue skim of light
coating his ankles and hands.
He pours a beer and watches

the stripped women dance on the screen.
My heart turns twice, nothing I ever wanted
in the dark room of time.

He sets his shoes in the kitchen. The bread box holds
wheat for the living, kolyva for the dead.
Once, I traded pure math for a blue-eyed husband.

We lived in a house that had stood vacant for a decade.
I took over the garden, took the wild gourds under
leaf, gathered water from the back river

that ran like a language behind the door.
A house is a scar
if you cannot sleep safe there:

what is broken, what survives.
Men who drink in bars
before breakfast use their hands

to show what cannot be said.
I call them
into the dark of the house.

Pink Dress

The hunters were my kin; with them, I shared a lineage.

Wake at night and the windows shine
with veins of neighboring highway;

put on the pink dress,
purchased at the thrift store by friends

who forgot how thin,
so the dress falls from shoulders;

nevertheless, put it on–uncles, grandfathers,
on both sides, were hunters, and knew the woods

for an inhuman place, a boundary.
Wear the pink dress, elusion,

where doorways merge with forest;
do not take it off, this redress

of language, married to sound without story,
woolen pink dress several sizes too large.

Maybe I will have to kneel,
but my name will be spoken:

the equations of winter
are hard that way.

Atonement: Mathematics

The apartment shared with my brother-in-law
got ruined by heavy weather.
Its nineteenth-century floorboards
later reclaimed for a luxury hotel.

The melancholy of mathematics:
that someone else always knows the answer.
Somewhere, the formula resolves itself,
the land's edge describes a curve

sounded by a vowel; given just one
consonant, it could be spoken as completion,
holding the floor of memory.
I should never have gone into words.

The ambiguity of what's spoken
has been too much for me.
But to stay with mathematics
and learn only what is already known,

even if known only by some future—a garden emptying
in empathy for ruined things, asymptotic vistas,
zero canceling every function it crosses.

Tift County, Georgia

Before winter turns, eleison
of vanishing birds—
killdeer, gray owl, and hawk,
the lanner, small and violent—

all turn inward toward some unspoken,
immemorial share. Grandfather of rain:
sweep red leaves from the house at dusk,
sweep roses, thorns, and kingdoms
from bedrooms through the front hallway

into Hall Avenue, shards of hickory, frangipani,
jacaranda, magnolia, spool of willow
as trains pull through.
Get rid of the dead for the living.

Afterimage

Before she was killed, my cousin might have walked to this clearing. A place in western Georgia untouched by fire, pine forest transiently owned by ancestors, most buried there. The places in foreign countries where our father took us without money; if I learned to beg in those rooms it was for sustenance like the untouched, original forest. Start over, with only the words of my eyes, verdance, stapled light between trees, fastening earth to sky. Breath by breath, the forest carries itself in time. Stand before the tables of strangers asking what I must, father's hands on my shoulders as I'd be his plough-horse through thickets, back in western Georgia. She might have led me to the place where horizon stills, a quieted fire, graves of the mound-builders. Her father among the lost, his gun that hit the mark.

Horseshoes

We played horseshoes in his yard that fall.
Harvest shallowed the fields.
Horseshoes' iron rang,
thrown with the force of will.

The song of their falling
could be autumn, tobacco harvest,
fine and super fine, graded leaves.
Before the small square house, polished

by sweeping, we threw horseshoes
left over from childhood horses we never rode,
empty harness of our mother's hearts.
Horseshoes carry sky or are carried by it:

the sound of their arc varies by target.
When they fall against moss and dirt,
it's the sigh of futility.
But when the shoe rocks against metal post,

it's an axe striking,
taking apart what must be burned to survive.
That year, we waited tables in town,
played horseshoes evenings afterwards,

by tobacco's golden vesture.
Fine and super fine; no matter the grade,
tobacco cannot survive damp.
The game of horseshoes begins and ends with luck.

We could be there still, throwing our chances.
Maybe he became a traveling salesman
riding between houses, a living ghost.
Maybe he granted at last the horses their rightful steps—

rust on our hands afterwards,
rust on all we touched.

Janitor

The year I worked as a janitor, it snowed every third day,
some stutter in the curve of tides.

To clean the emptied buildings of those you do not love,
shoulder all of winter:

go to the place where the cold hurts.
Through windows, shadows of kingfishers, tanagers,

caught my hands as I knelt to floors.
Against their shallow cries,

snow takes trees into its milk.
The year I worked as a janitor, I stopped being a pretty girl

and learned to touch the world,
at those parties where they want you but want nothing

to do with what you have cleaned.
Winter in New Haven, clean the haulm, humus, detritus

of forest, what comes in when the door's propped open.
When the boys pulled me in,

I shouldered the beauty of the rooms I had cleaned
unseen. The place of damage, winter

was my calling card;
walking late at night,

down blocks breathing traffic, vatic
cries of birds and engines. The world is a small drawing.

sets to its edge. So when the nightmares returned,
I took up this music swept thin.

Afterword

A PECULIAR GEOGRAPHY, the geography of losing and getting lost, typifies twenty-first century culture. How many of us now live in the same house, or the same neighborhood, or even the same town or city, in which our parents lived at the time of our birth? In which our grandparents and great-grandparents were born? As Gaston Bachelard, in *The Poetics of Space,* makes clear, the first house of childhood holds the shape of memory. And we have nearly all been dispossessed of the body of that memory. But for the incarcerated, the shape of the early house, the loss of that space, is a sharper, harsher, crueler and often absolute loss. Almost grotesque to compare the loss of access to place that is suffered by the incarcerated to the loss of access to one's first house suffered by the typical non-incarcerated 21st century American. And yet, we all, almost, know how it is. And then, really, we don't.

As a young teen, I spent roughly two months in solitary confinement; not for a crime but for responding to a troubled home in ways that—by many turns—landed me at the age of fourteen in solitary confinement. More than anything, I was considered stubborn and in need of "correcting." The place where this happened was a locked facility that claimed to offer treatment for wayward teens. Many of my adolescent compatriots there had committed petty, non-violent crimes. Others—like me—had committed no crime of any kind, only attempting to escape troubled families-of-origin situations with tactics that became truancy and run-away. No reason to say more except to note the absolute weirdness of one's relation to space caused by experiencing the entrapment of solitary confinement, especially at a young age. One never again feels the same about habitable man-made space. Habitable, man-made spaces, though, becomes one's obsession, as Merle Haggard once suggested when he said he felt at home on his tour bus because it reminded him of his prison cell. He was not joking; it is an odd reality that one becomes at home in enclosed spaces paradoxically for having once been confined. One becomes the space where one is held.

How to resist the shrinking of soul, keep the gaze of the hopeful child, looking at and looking for the corner of the world where one is safe, home, after surviving such a spatial violation? Here I do not mean the twisted sense of home to which Haggard referred but home as Bachelard would have it, the place of sky and earth at ease. The poems of *Ransom Street* tell about return after solitary confinement. If they are not poems of home they are poems of hope: of resilience, and the capacity to return, with love for the necessary beauty of sky and earth, love for those who harmed and made you, breath and matter, no matter what. ■

—Claire Millikin
Owls Head, Maine, 2018

Acknowledgments

An earlier version of "Atlantic" appeared in *CALYX*, as the 2015 Lois Prize recipient. ∎

About the Poet

PHOTO: Amy Wilton

CLAIRE MILLIKIN'S poetry has appeared in numerous literary journals and magazines, and she is the author of the poetry collections, *Tartessos and Other Cities (2016)*, *Television* (2016), *After Houses* (2014), *Motels Where We Lived* (2014), *Museum Of Snow* (2013). She received her BA in philosophy from Yale University, MFA in poetry from New York University, and PhD in English literature from the Graduate Center of the City University of New York. Millikin currently teaches art history and sociology, as a lecturer at the University of Virginia, Charlottesville. www.claireraymond.org. ∎

Other Books By 2Leaf Press

2Leaf Press challenges the status quo by publishing alternative fiction, non-fiction, poetry and bilingual works by activists, academics, poets and authors dedicated to diversity and social justice with scholarship that is accessible to the general public. 2Leaf Press produces high quality and beautifully produced hardcover, paperback and ebook formats through our series: 2LP Explorations in Diversity, 2LP University Books, 2LP Classics, 2LP Translations, Nuyorican World Series, and 2LP Current Affairs, Culture & Politics. Below is a selection of 2Leaf Press' published titles.

2LP EXPLORATIONS IN DIVERSITY

Substance of Fire: Gender and Race in the College Classroom
by Claire Millikin
Foreword by R. Joseph Rodríguez, Afterword by Richard Delgado
Contributors Riley Blanks, Blake Calhoun, Rox Trujillo

Black Lives Have Always Mattered
A Collection of Essays, Poems, and Personal Narratives
Edited by Abiodun Oyewole

The Beiging of America:
Personal Narratives about Being Mixed Race in the 21st Century
Edited by Cathy J. Schlund-Vials, Sean Frederick Forbes, Tara Betts
Afterword by Heidi Durrow

What Does it Mean to be White in America?
Breaking the White Code of Silence, A Collection of Personal Narratives
Edited by Gabrielle David and Sean Frederick Forbes
Introduction by Debby Irving, Afterword by Tara Betts

2LP UNIVERSITY BOOKS
Designs of Blackness
Mappings in the Literature and Culture of African Americans
by A. Robert Lee
20TH ANNIVERSARY EXPANDED EDITION

2LP CLASSICS
Adventures in Black and White
by Philippa Schuyler
Edited and with a critical introduction by Tara Betts

Monsters: Mary Shelley's Frankenstein and Mathilda
by Mary Shelley, edited by Claire Millikin Raymond

2LP TRANSLATIONS
Birds on the Kiswar Tree
by Odi Gonzales, translated by Lynn Levin
Bilingual: English/Spanish

Incessant Beauty, A Bilingual Anthology
by Ana Rossetti, edited and translated by Carmela Ferradáns
Bilingual: English/Spanish

NUYORICAN WORLD SERIES
*Entre el sol y la nieve: escritos de fin de siglo / Between the Sun and
Snow: Writing at the End of the Century*
by Myna Nieves, translated by Christopher Hirschmann Brandt
Bilingual: English/Spanish

Our Nuyorican Thing, The Birth of a Self-Made Identity
by Samuel Carrion Diaz, Introduction by Urayoán Noel

*Hey Yo! Yo Soy!, 40 Years of Nuyorican Street Poetry,
The Collected Works of Jesús Papoleto Meléndez*
Bilingual: English/Spanish

LITERARY NONFICTION
No Vacancy; Homeless Women in Paradise
by Michael Reid

The Beauty of Being, A Collection of Fables, Short Stories & Essays
by Abiodun Oyewole

WHEREABOUTS: Stepping Out of Place,
An Outside in Literary & Travel Magazine Anthology
Edited by Brandi Dawn Henderson

ESSAYS
The Emergence of Ecosocialism, Collected Essays by Joel Kovel
Edited by Quincy Saul

PLAYS
Rivers of Women, The Play
by Shirley Bradley LeFlore, photographs by Michael J. Bracey

AUTOBIOGRAPHIES/MEMOIRS/BIOGRAPHIES
An Unintentional Accomplice:
A Personal Perspective on White Responsibility
by Carolyn L. Baker

Trailblazers, Black Women Who Helped Make America Great
American Firsts/American Icons, Vols. 1 and 2
by Gabrielle David, Introduction by Chandra D. L. Waring
Edited by Carolina Fung Feng

Mother of Orphans
The True and Curious Story of Irish Alice, A Colored Man's Widow
by Dedria Humphries Barker
Introduction by Cathy J. Schlund-Vials

Strength of Soul
by Naomi Raquel Enright

Dream of the Water Children:
Memory and Mourning in the Black Pacific
by Fredrick D. Kakinami Cloyd
Foreword by Velina Hasu Houston, Introduction by Gerald Horne
Edited by Karen Chau

The Fourth Moment: Journeys from the Known to the Unknown, A Memoir
by Carole J. Garrison, Introduction by Sarah Willis

POETRY

Ransom Street, Poems by Claire Millikin
Introduction by Kathleen Ellis

Wounds Fragments Derelict, Poems by Carlos Gabriel Kelly
Introduction by Sean Frederick Forbes

PAPOLíTICO, Poems of a Political Persuasion
by Jesús Papoleto Meléndez
with an Introduction by Joel Kovel and DeeDee Halleck

Critics of Mystery Marvel, Collected Poems
by Youssef Alaoui, Introduction by Laila Halaby

shrimp
by jason vasser-elong, Introduction by Michael Castro

The Revlon Slough, New and Selected Poems
by Ray DiZazzo, Introduction by Claire Millikin

A Country Without Borders: Poems and Stories of Kashmir
by Lalita Pandit Hogan, Introduction by Frederick Luis Aldama

2Leaf Press Inc. is a nonprofit organization that publishes and promotes
multicultural literature.

FLORIDA ■ NEW YORK
www.2leafpress.org